EVERYDAY ECONOMICS
INVESTING

Jessica Morrison

Weigl Publishers Inc.

Published by Weigl Publishers Inc.
350 5th Avenue, Suite 3304, PMB 6G
New York, NY 10118-0069

Website: www.weigl.com

Library of Congress Cataloging-in-Publication Data available upon request.
Fax 1-866-44-WEIGL for the attention of the Publishing Records department.

ISBN 978-1-60596-649-6 (hard cover)
ISBN 978-1-60596-650-2 (soft cover)

Printed in China
1 2 3 4 5 6 7 8 9 0 13 12 11 10 09

Every reasonable effort has been made to trace ownership and to obtain permission to reprint
copyright material. The publishers would be pleased to have any errors or omissions brought
to their attention so that they may be corrected in subsequent printings.

Weigl acknowledges Getty Images as its primary image supplier for this title.

Project Coordinator **Heather C. Hudak** I Designer **Terry Paulhus** I Layout **Kenzie Browne**

All of the Internet URLs given in the book were valid at the time of publication. However, due to the dynamic
nature of the Internet, some addresses may have changed, or sites may have ceased to exist since publication.
While the author and publisher regret any inconvenience this may cause readers, no responsibility for any such

CONTENTS

INVESTING VOCABULARY

MUTUAL FUNDS a type of investment that pools together the money of many people and spreads it among a variety of stocks and bonds; mutual funds are managed by professionals

RETURN how much money a person gets back from an initial investment

RISK uncertainty that an investment will gain money; typically, a risky investment is one that may gain large sums of money if successful or lose some, or all, of the money if it is not

STOCKS pieces, or shares, of a company a person can buy, represented by a certificate

What is Investing?

Investing is a system of putting money into a company, bank, or organization in the hope that it will be worth more in the future. In other words, an investment is anything a person buys that may become more valuable over time. It is a way of making a **return** on the money a person has. When people invest, they give money to someone else to make more money. For example, a person might give a company $1,000 for startup costs. In exchange, the company gives the person a percentage of its earnings. This is an investment.

In order to invest, a person must save money. Saving is a way storing money in a safe place, such as a bank account. Some of the money a person saves can be invested. There are several investing options, such as **stocks** and **mutual funds**.

People often invest their money to save for the future.

When people make investments, they are taking a **risk** with their money. Different types of investments have varying amounts of risk and returns. The key to investing well is to minimize the risk and maximize the return.

Investing can be thought of like the peaks and valleys of a mountain range. Sometimes, investments increase and are worth more money. Other times, there are dips in the value of the investment, and it is worth less money.

People can receive advice from investment advisors about the best ways to grow their money.

When Did Investing Begin?

Throughout history, investments have helped shape money management around the world.

1606 The oldest known stock certificate is issued for a Dutch company, Vereinigte Oostindische Compaignie, that is involved with the spice trade in India.

1789–1795 Alexander Hamilton, the first U.S. Secretary of the Treasury, promotes the development of the American stock exchange.

1790 The U.S. federal government issues $80 million in **bonds** from Revolutionary War debt. These bonds are traded publicly, and the U.S. investment markets are born.

1606   1789-1795   1790

1792 Twenty-four of New York's leading merchants and businesspeople sign the Buttonwood Agreement. This agreement officially founds the New York Stock and Exchange Board.

1815 After the War of 1812, the **stock exchange** begins to grow. Bonds, as well as bank and insurance stocks, are traded.

1844 The **telegraph** is invented. **Brokers** and investors who live outside of Manhattan participate more in investing because they can communicate more easily.

1863 The New York Stock and Exchange Board is given a new name. It is now known as the New York Stock Exchange (NYSE).

1867 The world's first stock **ticker** is invented by Edward A. Calahan. It displays the current stock prices.

1914 During World War I, trading of investments stops around the world. It is the longest exchange shutdown in history, lasting 4.5 months.

1929 Many investors lose money in the **Great Depression**.

1954 "Own Your Share of American Business" is launched at the NYSE to raise awareness of investing throughout the United States.

2007 The New York Stock Exchange breaks records, handling 4,121,107,134 shares in a single day.

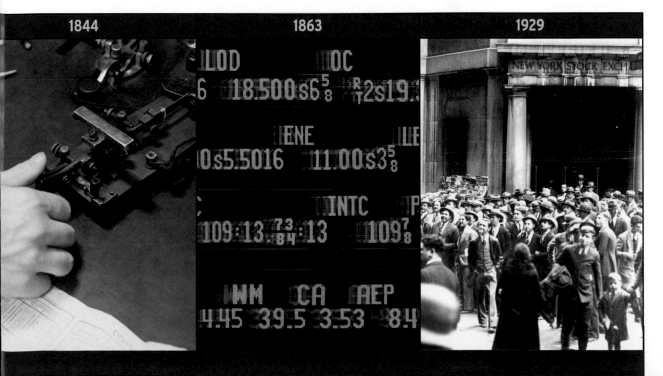

1844   1863   1929

Investing in the United States

In 1531, Belgium founded one of the world's first stock exchanges. Amsterdam soon followed, opening the world's first public bank in 1609. Paris and London had their own stock exchanges around this time as well. Many of the exchanges were related to the spice trade.

When the idea of investing money came to the United States in the 1700s, Boston and Philadelphia were major centers of financial activity. Bonds for road and bridge projects were sold, along with contracts for goods, such as molasses. People soon wanted an official place to do their financial **trading**. At the time, New York was the nation's capital, and Alexander Hamilton was the Secretary of the Treasury.

OCK EXCHANGE

The New York Stock Exchange is located on Wall Street.

Hamilton believed that stock exchanges were an important part of building a good **economy**.

In 1792, John Sutton, Benjamin Jay, and 22 other New York City brokers met under a buttonwood tree in what is now Battery Park, New York. They signed a contract, later known as the Buttonwood Agreement. This contract officially established an investing organization, called The Stock Exchange Office. Later, the name was changed to the New York Stock Exchange. It was located on Wall Street in Lower Manhattan, New York.

Investing in the United States had a modest start but grew quickly. Today, it is a fast-paced, booming business, and Wall Street is known around the world. There are several other stock exchanges as well, and people can use computers to invest their money quickly and easily.

░FAQ

What is the difference between the bid price and the ask price?
The bid price is the amount of money a person is prepared to pay for a certain investment. The ask price is the amount the seller wants to be paid for the investment.

What is investment income?
Investment income is the money earned from interest and profits on all of the investments owned by a person or company, or money gained from the sale of any investments.

INVESTING VOCABULARY

BALANCE the amount of money in an account

DEBT INVESTMENTS loaning money, which earns interest; debt investments must be paid back by those who borrow the money

EQUITY INVESTMENTS loaning money to a person or business for a share of the money it makes; the lender is not guaranteed to be paid back for equity investments

FEES the prices paid for services

INTEREST a percentage of the money that a bank or organization pays a person for investing with it

INVESTMENT PERIOD the length of time it should take for an investment to achieve the desired results

How Does Investing Work?

There are a few ways for investments to make money. Some investments earn **interest**. Other investments are purchased at a low price and sold at a higher price for a profit. Some investments allow the purchaser to own a piece of a company, gaining a percentage of that company's earnings over time.

There are many types of investments. Each has different terms and features, so people must decide which investments best suit their needs. In general, investments are either **debt investments** or **equity investments**.

Short-term investments include bank account savings, certificates of deposit (CDs), and treasury bills. These are debt investments that reach the end of their **investment period** in a short time.

Putting money in a simple bank account is a basic way to invest money for future use. Monthly statements show the **balance**, interest earned, and **fees**. Money in a savings account can be accessed any time.

Treasury bills reach the end of their investment period in less than one year. CDs usually reach the end of their term in one month to five years. The government guarantees these investments, so they are fairly safe. However, they earn a lower rate of interest than equity investments.

Elements of Investing

There are three basic elements involved in investing money. The money earned on an investment will depend on these factors.

Time
Some investments require only a few months to increase, while others make take more than 30 years to make a significant return.

Capital
Capital refers to the money a person has available to put toward a new project, such as investments.

Growth Rate
The growth rate refers to how quickly an investment will grow over time. All investments have different growth rates. The growth rate of an investment can change over time, depending on the type of investment.

INVESTING VOCABULARY

DEFAULTING when a company does not make payments to an investor as outlined by a contract

DIVERSIFY to spread out money among many different investments; diversifying is much safer than investing in one opportunity

FOREIGN CURRENCY money from another country

SHARES portions of a company

Types of Investments

Before making an investment, many people research the types of investments that are available. This helps them make a well-informed choice about how to invest their money.

Bonds

When money is loaned to a company, it is called a bond. Bonds are a kind of equity investment. The company that received the loan is expected to pay back the full amount borrowed, as well as a certain amount of interest, by a specific deadline. Bonds normally are paid back between 10 and 30 years. Bonds give a slightly higher interest rate compared to short-term investments. When a bond issuer fails to make payments, it is called **defaulting**.

Stocks

Stocks are **shares** of a company. When people buy shares from a company, they become shareholders.

Money is invested in a variety of products, such as gold, oil, and cattle.

This means that they own part of that company. When people are shareholders of companies that make money, their stocks increase in value. If the company loses money, the value of the stock decreases. Stocks are never guaranteed, and they often increase and decrease in value. People can make a great deal of money if they buy shares at a low price and sell them at a high price. Investing in the stock market requires assistance from a broker working at a stock exchange.

Mutual Funds

Sometimes, many investors pool together their money to buy different types of investments. These mutual funds are used to buy stocks and bonds, such as CDs, treasury bonds, real estate, gold, and **foreign** **currency**. Mutual funds are popular because they allow investors to **diversify**. By doing this, there is less chance of losing large sums of money if one stock decreases in value. Another stock might increase, balancing the loss.

Commodities and Untraditional Investments

Many people invest their money in items they believe will increase in value over time. Gold, oil, or products such as meat and soybeans are examples. The prices of these items are driven by supply and demand. This means that the price for these products will increase if many people want to buy them.

Why Should
a Person Invest?

Advisors are people who can provide information about different types of investments. They help people make investment choices that are best-suited to their personal needs and decrease unnecessary risk. Investing can help people prepare for future expenses, stay ahead of **inflation**, and reach their financial goals.

Items that once cost a single dollar may now cost several dollars. This is called inflation. Inflation happens over time as prices increase. Investing money helps people keep up with this rising cost of buying food, homes, and general goods and services. For example, in 1886, a serving of Coca Cola™ cost five cents. Today, it costs a dollar or more.

Investments can help pay for long-term goals, such as retirement, vacations, and property.

There are two main types of financial goals. Short-term goals are items that people want to purchase in the near future, such as a bike or MP3 player. Long-term goals are items that people hope to purchase years into the future. Buying a house, going to college, or traveling the world are all long-term goals. Eventually, people wish to stop working for a living. Retirement is another long-term goal most people share. Money saved through investing can help people finance their expenses during retirement.

The goal of all investments is to allow a person to earn more money using the money that person already has. The earlier people begin investing, the more money they can make.

::FAQ

What does it mean to have a stock portfolio?

A portfolio is a group of different types of investments, such as stocks and bonds, that are owned by one person or company.

What do the terms overweight, equal weight, and underweight mean?

A stock is overweight when it is deemed to have a better value than similar stocks. When a stock is underweight, it has a lesser value than similar stocks. Equal weight is when all stocks in the portfolio have the same importance.

Wall Street and the New York Stock Exchange

When investing first began in the United States, many big changes were happening in the country. In 1653, Dutch settlers built a large wall on the lower end of Manhattan, New York, to protect people against British attacks and other dangers. The path along this wall became known as Wall Street. Before an official stock exchange was established, businesspeople would gather along Wall Street to buy and sell parts of companies. When it first became used for stock and bond exchanges, Wall Street was only a few blocks of unpaved road.

After the Buttonwood Agreement was signed in 1792, Wall Street became famous around the world as the center of commerce in the United States.

Information about investments is posted on screens throughout the New York Stock Exchange.

Businesspeople and stock brokers moved into a building on Wall Street and began trading there. Wall Street became known around the world as the center of **commerce** in the United States.

Before 1792, if businesspeople wanted to make investments, they had to place an advertisement in the paper or speak with their friends. After the Stock Exchange Office was established, people had a safe, secure way of investing. In the 1800s, Wall Street offered investments from about 20 **publicly traded** corporations. Today, the New York Stock Exchange lists thousands of companies available for investing.

In the early 1900s, many people made fortunes in the stock market. However, in 1929, there was a stock market crash that caused millions of people to lose their money.

⁞FAQ

What do the words bear and bull mean in the stock market?

The words "bear" and "bull" are used to describe the current stock market, as well as individual brokers. A bull market is one that is rising, while a bear market is one in which prices are falling. Likewise, a bull is someone who thinks the prices will rise, and a bear believes they will fall. There are many theories as to how these investing terms first came into use. The first published book to use them was written by Thomas Mortimer in 1775.

Behind the Scenes

What happens when you invest in mutual funds?

1 When people invest in mutual funds, they give their money to a company that they trust to make investments for them.

2 The mutual fund company pools the money with that of other investors. People who manage funds invest this pooled money in a variety of stocks, bonds, or both.

3 If the various investments increase in value, the mutual fund also grows.

4 The investor receives a proportional share of the profits, determined by the number of shares invested.

Stock Market Signals

When trading first began on the New York Stock Exchange, stock brokers would stand on the street corner yelling out bids on shares. Soon, a system of hand gestures was developed because there was too much noise. Although many brokers still shout out their bids, the system of hand signals is used in some exchanges.

Sell: Hands pushing away from body with palms facing outward

Buy: Hands pulling forward in front of body with palms facing inward

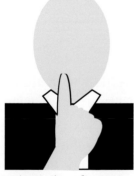

One: Index finger touches chin

Twenty: Index and middle finger touch forehead

Hundred: Clenched fist is held upright

What is Liquidity?

Investment liquidity refers to how quickly people can access their money to use for purchases. In other words, an investment that is liquid can be accessed very quickly. An investment with little liquidity takes more time to access. In this type of investment, there is a great deal of paperwork, many phone calls, and other steps needed before a person can access the money.

It may be helpful to think of investments like water. The more liquid the investments are, the more easily they flow like water. Large investments, such as stocks, can be thought of as ice. The money is available, but it cannot be used until it becomes liquid. When people talk about liquidity, they are referring to **converting** their investments into money that can be used immediately.

Liquid money is not tied up in investments and can be accessed quickly for use.

Money invested in a savings account usually is quite liquid. It can be accessed fairly easily through a bank **teller** or **Automated Teller Machine** (ATM). This money can be used immediately to make purchases.

Stocks and bonds have very little liquidity. Money invested in stocks and bonds can be accessed only after a certain time has passed. Leaving money in stocks and bonds for a longer period of time will allow them to gain as much money as possible. The benefits of investing are lost by removing money before it has a chance to grow.

ATMs can be found in many places, including stores, banks, restaurants, and on street corners.

Reading Your Investments

Stock market numbers are displayed on TV and in newspapers. This helps people decide whether to buy or sell their stocks. One of the best-known stock price lists is the **Dow Jones Industrial Average**. For more than 100 years, the Dow Jones has published the prices of large company stocks. A group of 30 stocks are **averaged** each day, resulting in the Dow Jones Industrial Average.

Another well-known stock market tracker is the **Standard and Poor's 500 Index (S&P 500)**. Tracking 500 different stocks, the S&P 500 gives a fairly broad picture of the stock market and is used by many mutual fund managers. Both the Dow Jones and S&P 500 Index are referenced daily by many investors. Many investors use more than one market indicator to track their stocks.

Stocks

This chart shows how to read a stock report.

The YTD, or year-to-date, percentage change tells the difference between today's price and the price at the beginning of the year. This positive value means that the current price is 14.97 percent higher than the price earlier in the year.

The Net Chg, or net change, of the stock compares the most recent price of the stock with the last displayed price. A positive value of 0.20 means that $15.00 is 0.20 cents higher than the stock price from the day before.

YTD % CHG	52-Weeks HI	LO	Stock	SYMB	Last	Net Chg
+14.97	21.0	4.0	Business	BUSI	15.00	+0.20

52-Weeks High/Low numbers are the higheset and lowest prices the stock has sold at throughout a whole year. At its lowest point, this stock sold for $4.00 a share. At its highest, it sold for $21.00.

Every company that sells its stock is represented by a symbol. This is called the Symb. Typically, the stock symbol is the first few letters of the company name.Stock refers to the type of company or its name.

Last refers to the most recent price of the stock from the day before, as it was displayed in the stock report.

Bonds

When people buy bonds, they are lending money to a company. Like stock reports, bond tables can be difficult to understand. This chart shows how to read a bond table.

Coupon is the fixed interest rate the company will pay a person for buying a bond.

Bid $ is the price a person will pay for the bond. It is a percentage in relation to 100, so a bid of 98.5 is 98.5 percent. If a bond is bought for $100, a bid of 50% means someone is willing to pay $50 for it.

	Coupon	Mat. Date	Bid $	Yld %
Corporate				
BUSI	7.200	Sep 10/25	98.50	9.75

Corporate refers to the company that is issuing the bond.

Maturity Date is when the borrower will repay the sum of the money that was borrowed initially. Normally, the last two numbers of the year are displayed.

Yield is the yearly return in a percentage until the bond matures.

INVESTING VOCABULARY

COMPOUNDING the growth that comes from an investment when earnings build upon themselves

How Much Money Can Investing Make?

The amount of money people make through investing depends on many factors. How much money is initially invested, as well as how long the investment is left to grow, both affect the profit. The growth rate of interest can drastically affect the return.

Some investments make money through **compounding**. After one year, a $100 investment with a 10 percent growth rate of interest would earn $10. This is added to the initial investment for a new total of $110. After another year, 10 percent of the new total, or $11, will be added to the balance of the investment, for a new total of $121.

■ Saved money can add up over time.

This continues for the time the money remains invested. At this rate, the money will double after eight years. When money is compounded, the amount by which it grows over time increases more rapidly.

Different types of investments have different growth rates. A bank account or certificate of deposit might earn a five percent interest rate. This is similar to the rate of interest on some bonds. Stock market investments grow each year. For most of the past century, the average growth rate on the stock market was 11 percent. Some companies earn up to 15 percent.

Dividing the number 72 by the rate of interest an investment receives will show how long it will take to double the money in an investment. This is called the Rule of 72.

⊞FAQ

How much interest will a person earn on $100?

Starting with $100, the money a person earns on an investment can vary greatly, depending on the type of investment. This graph shows different rates of interest over a certain number of years.

Number of years	Interest rate		
	5%	11%	15%
5	$128	$169	$201
10	$163	$284	$405
15	$208	$478	$814
20	$265	$806	$1637
25	$339	$1359	$3292
30	$432	$2289	$6621

Investing Technology

Technology plays a major role in modern investing. One of the best-known examples of investing technology was launched in 1971. The National Association of Securities Dealers Automated Quotations (NASDAQ) is an electronic stock market that helps people buy and sell their investments. This computerized system allows stocks to be traded electronically. When the NASDAQ was first invented, stock trading happened using a computer bulletin board system and telephones. This continued for 20 years, until technology advanced. Today, stock prices can be viewed on a stock ticker. The NASDAQ also creates reports on the number of daily trades.

The Internet has made it possible to keep track of several investment opportunities at a moment's notice. There are many websites that constantly track investment information from around the world.

Careers in Investing

There are many different investing jobs.
These are just a few examples.

Stock Brokers

Stock brokers are professionals who help people with the process of investing money. They buy and sell investment shares, working within the guidelines of the stock exchange. A stock broker can work for a large company or an individual person. Most stock brokers enjoy math, economics, and business. They attend college to study in one or more of these areas. Stock brokers must pass the General Securities Registered Representative Examination to become licensed. After passing this exam, a person becomes a trainee. Stock brokers gain much of their experience through on-the-job training at an investing firm. They are expected to take courses and training to keep their skills sharp. It is important for stock brokers to enjoy working in a fast-paced environment.

Registered Investment Advisor

Investment advisors help people make suitable investment decisions so they can reach their financial goals. To do this, it is important that an investment advisor ask about income and the risk a person is comfortable taking. Some advisors work for banks, while others start their own firms or work within a company. Investment advisors must take financial planning courses and become registered by the Securities and Exchange Commission. They must be knowledgeable in all areas of money-management, as well as the investing industry. It is good for investment advisors to enjoy working with people because they spend a great deal of time interacting and communicating with clients.

What Have You Learned?

1 What is investing?

2 Name three types of investments.

3 When was the Buttonwood Agreement signed?

4 What is the NASDAQ?

5 What is a mutual fund?

6 Why is diversifying important when investing?

7 What is Wall Street?

8 How does a debt investment differ from an equity investment?

9 What is a risk?

10 What is inflation?

Answers

1. the act of putting money into a company, bank, or other organization, in hope that it will be worth more someday

2. stocks, bonds, mutual funds, and commodities

3. 1792

4. an electronic stock market, where the trading of stocks takes place

5. an investment which pools the money of many people together, investing it in several different options

6. Diversifying helps people even out the highs and lows of their investments, making them more money overall.

7. a place in Manhattan, New York, where the New York Stock Exchange was established

8. A debt investment must be paid back after a certain time. Equity investments are much riskier and do not require the investor to be paid back.

9. the potential for investors to lose some, or all, of their money in an investment

10. the rising cost of living over time

29

Make a Mock Stock Portfolio

Before investing money, it is a good idea to practice building a mock portfolio for stocks.

1. Begin by making a list of the companies in which you would like to invest. This may include your favorite restaurants or stores.

2. Once you have completed the list of companies, find their stock prices on the Internet. Beside each company on your list, write down the price of its stock.

3. Imagine you have bought 100 shares of stock from each company you have listed. Now, you have a mock stock portfolio that you can track daily.

4. Check the prices of your stock each day for a month. Has your stock increased or decreased in price?

5. Watch the latest news for information about the companies from which you have chosen to buy stock. Have any of the companies been featured in a positive or negative way? Has this affected the price of their stock? Once you have practiced with a mock portfolio, you may wish to begin investing some real money.

Further Research

Many books and websites provide information on banking. To learn more about banking, borrow books from the library, or surf the Internet.

Most libraries have computers that connect to a database for researching information. If you input a key word, you will be provided with a list of books in the library that contain information on that topic. Nonfiction books are arranged numerically, using their call number. Fiction books are organized alphabetically by the author's last name.

Websites

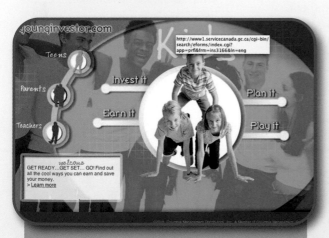

Learn all about investing at

**www.younginvestor.com/
kids/**

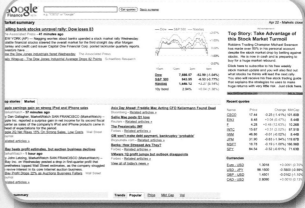

Search the current price
of stocks at

www.google.com/finance

Glossary

Automated Teller Machine: a machine that can provide basic banking services, such as providing cash

averaged: several quantities are added together and then the total is divided by the number of quantities

balance: the amount of money in an account

bonds: money a person lends to a company that earns more money over time

brokers: people who buy and sell goods on behalf of other people

commerce: the act of large-scale buying and selling

compounding: the growth that comes from an investment when earnings build upon themselves

converting: causing change

debt investment: loaning money, which earns interest; debt investments must be paid back by those who borrow the money

defaulting: when a company does not make payments to an investor as outlined by a contract

diversify: to spread out money among many different investments; diversifying is much safer than investing in one opportunity

Dow Jones Industrial Average: an indicator of stock exchange prices, based on 30 companies

economy: the wealth and resources of a nation or a certain place; the supply and demand of goods and services

equity investments: loaning money to someone else for a share of the money they make with it; the lender is not guaranteed to be paid back for equity investments

fees: the prices paid for services

foreign currency: money from another country

Great Depression: after the stock market crash of 1929, a period of financial lows in the 1930s

inflation: the rising cost of goods and services over time

interest: a percentage of the money that a bank or organization pays a person for investing with them

investment period: the length of time it should take for an investment to achieve the desired results

mutual funds: a type of investment that pools together the money of many people, and spreads it among a variety of stocks and bonds; mutual funds are managed by professionals

publicly traded: a company that has shares being traded in the stock market

return: how much money a person gets back from an initial investment

risk: uncertainty that an investment will gain value; typically, a risky investment is one that may gain large sums of money if successful or lose some, or all, of the money if it is not

shares: portions of a company

Standard and Poor's 500 Index: an indicator of stock exchange prices, based on 500 different organizations

stock exchange: a place where stock shares are bought and sold

stocks: pieces, or shares, of a company a person can buy, represented by a certificate

telegraph: a system for sending long-distance messages

teller: a person who makes transactions in a bank

ticker: a device that displays current information in real time

trading: the buying and selling of stocks by a stock broker

Index